Letting Go

poems by

Holly Norton

Finishing Line Press
Georgetown, Kentucky

Letting Go

ACKNOWLEDGMENTS

"Tijuana" was a finalist for the Fall 2015 Orlando Prize from A Room of Her
Own Foundation

Many thanks to the Community of Writers for their valuable feedback.

Publisher: Leah Maines

Editor: Christen Kincaid

Cover Art: Barbara Spurgeon

Author Photo: Barbara Spurgeon

Cover Design: Elizabeth Maines McCleavy

Printed in the USA on acid-free paper.
Order online: www.finishinglinepress.com
also available on amazon.com

Author inquiries and mail orders:
Finishing Line Press
P. O. Box 1626
Georgetown, Kentucky 40324
U. S. A.

Table of Contents

For my mother

Tijuana

Southern California unwinds like a filmstrip
Unreels when we cross the border in the mint green Edsel
Men run into the street to meet my father and me
Wave their arms and say, "Senor! Senorita!"
He gets out to make a deal
Fifty dollars for new upholstery
Twenty for a new set of rims
He ends with a joke about us getting married
They laugh. I look at the ground.

On the street I look at the pinatas and sombreros
Embroidered with the name of the city
Serapes woven with yarn in colors not found in nature
My father sees a purse like his cowboy boots,
Ostrich skin with dimples where their feathers were plucked
Like the pimples pushing through my skin
And the hairs above my lip that I'm starting to pull out with
Tweezers like tiny forceps.

He sees me eyeing a silver bracelet inset with abalone flowers
Says to the cashier, "She'll take this one,"
Slams it on the glass counter
I flinch
He pays for it
Clamps it to my wrist.

We walk past darkened bars
Disinfectant wafting from open doors
But my father buys his tequila on the street
Where we eat tacos full of meat and beans
Let the juice dribble into the wrappers and down our arms
And don't speak.

Going back we see a man
With no hands and no feet
He sits on a cart with a can that says, "Please"
I reach down, and my bracelet sounds like
Money in his cup
My father walks on.

Sorting

You decided to drive to the place where he died in case you wanted
        to bring back anything
Take time adjusting to your father being gone along with any chance
        of ever really knowing him
His death sudden—first a fall, then surgery, then infection
You leave from Lenexa, pass through Wichita, Albuquerque, arrive in
Santa Ana
To find a mess that you didn't expect
From a man who once stated
        that he kept his place immaculate
Layers of dust showing years of neglect
Food in the fridge past its "sell by" date
Nothing to show that he had any hope
Nothing you want besides the shotgun
        you can add to your collection
You think of his refusal to accept any gift
Angry denial that he needed anything , that it would just go to waste
The bottles and cigarette cartons on the floor seem to look up and say,
        We've seen this before.

Dollhouse

It was made of metal,
Red brick and bushes stamped on the front,
The back open for inspection.
I used to imagine a family living there,
A father who never lost his temper,
A mother who never made the children stay outside while he
        was sleeping off a hangover.
I used to imagine the rooms filled with furniture,
        dressers and beds, maybe even a vanity,
But there were only painted windows, floors,
        and walls,
Reminders of the boxes where we kept our voices.

Clothing Optional

When I was three,
You would put clothes on me.
I would take them off at the first opportunity,
Run giggling through the yard, down the street,
Chubby legs propelling me sometimes as far
      as the Catholic Church on the corner.

You ran after me, laughing, too.
I imagine the people who saw me and you wondering why
      that mother couldn't keep clothes on her daughter,
You wondering why you should bother.

Going Back

I used to say, we went way back,
As far as we could go.
I never asked you about my birth,
What it was like to push me out
        of the plush home you had furnished for me.
You only said that I was perfect, a "7-11."
I thought of convenience stores and Slurpees.

What was it like for you to know
        that you were giving my brother a sister
A daughter to a man who had trouble holding his liquor
        and his temper?
You only knew you would protect her,
Shelter her from the storm of his rage,
That she would have a love of the page that you did
        as a girl.

The Break

Remember when we used to ride our bikes to the Catholic church
in Lomita?
We circled the fountain with Mary in the middle
Went to the window to see the nuns
They gave us their leftover donuts.
One day I found a bracelet on the ground, took it to the window,
and let the nuns know.
They told me keep it.
Later I wondered if they planted it.

Then there were times I'd ride my bike to the drugstore on the
other side of Pacific Coast Highway
Feeling so grownup and independent
I never noticed how you were always there
looking at the cheap plastic toys with me
Helping me see what I could afford.

We raked leaves that fell from the fig tree,
Scraped off the fruit that stuck to our shoes
Digged in the dirt for worms and ate sour grass
Looked for the rabbit living under the shed,
Tried to keep quiet when Dad was home from third shift or
sleeping off a night at the bar

That day when you were playing darts
I walked by just as one made its arc toward the board
You're the one who got the spanking for that
You were the star pitcher of the Little League
I skipped rope to get a present from Dad for every hundred jumps.
Then came the day after Christmas.
Mom told us Dad would be living somewhere else.
She got a job driving a bus
We became "latchkey kids" from a "broken home."
The break mended me, but something broke in you,
trapped in a house with two women
no father figure to give you direction.

Christmas Gifts

The day after Christmas,
You told us our dad would no longer live with us
I stood there in my pink flame-retardant pjs,
Clutched my new Baby Tender Love
Looked at my brother to make sure I'd heard right
Realized that I was finally free.

No more demands for silence to sleep off the third shift or a night
at the bar
Other kids could come over when they wanted to
Even the Okies and the Jehovah's Witnesses
No more taking the belt from the shelf then folding it in half
Before the crack

You were a divorcee, we were latchkey kids from a broken home
We walked home alone, let ourselves in, made "potions" out of
anything we could find in the
kitchen—baking soda, vinegar, cream of tartar
Watched cartoons while we waited for you to come home from a
day of driving the short bus.
You told us tales of children who lived in cardboard boxes, a boy
who had to be wrapped in
batting, his nerves on the surface of his skin.

Dad had visitation. Every weekend, he would pick us up in his
orange Renault, and
We would go with him
Sometimes to the pier, where he would buy us smoked salmon
Sometimes bowling. Over and over, my ball would land in the
gutter
Dad saw my careless shrug and coached me, like he did from the
bleachers
at my brother's baseball games
I pretended to listen but didn't care.

You heard the call of your hometown in Iowa
And the family business, swimming pool construction
An irony if there ever was one
Dad bought us kids first-class tickets
You took a U-Haul from California to Iowa
Almost washing off the road in a desert downpour
But making it to Des Moines, our furniture and dog intact

That apartment was too small for the three of us
The brother who was missing a father figure,
The sister who couldn't fit in at school,
The mother trying to make ends meet.
Eviction was a foregone conclusion.

Then the move to the trailer across town
A tin can, as you called it
Where we could yell without the neighbors hearing it
Or at least not being able to do anything about it
As long as we were inside
And had a dog we had no idea how to train

Breathing Room

What must it have been like to wake up breathless
Not with anticipation
With lack of oxygen
The panic sets in
You call 911
Gasp for breath and wait for them to come.

Medics arrive
Place a mask on your face
Take you away without a change of clothes
No siren, only the sound of wheels on the road
Take you to a place where you know you will have to do
        what they tell you.

Then to a room with a bed on wheels
Fluorescent lights buzz, dilate your eyes
Vicks Vapo Rub wafts through the air
They take you out of your t-shirt you slept in
Put you in a gown that you can't tie around you
Help you crawl under the sheets pulled so tight
You wonder if you will stop breathing again

It's morning and another inmate comes in
Pleasant enough, with talk about the weather
Her daughter coming to visit her
Only later do you learn her reason for being there
Chronic incontinence
You eat the flavorless meat and pudding that only those with no
choice
        will tolerate in this salt- and caffeine-free facility
You finally coax a shaker and a diet cola from a sympathetic nurse

They let you go and now you tell me
There's no place like the hospital to make you appreciate home
The nurse comes a few times a week, and
Your meals are on wheels
I imagine you trying to catch them, gasping for air,
Helpless, as I am now.

Letting Go

First—Chill—then Stupor—then the letting go—
Emily Dickinson, *"After great pain, a formal feeling comes"*

Where did you go before you left?
When you couldn't speak but made yourself say,
"I'm dying. Let me go."
I told you to try as hard as you could
To live so that you could stay with me
When I finally told you it was o.k. to go
That I was taking you to a place where you
Would be unplugged from all the tubes
You put your hand on mine
Squeezed it as hard as you could
As if to say *thank you.*

How many times did you let me go?
When I was learning how to ride a bike,
First with training wheels, then with none,
You watched me teeter,
Resisted the urge to hold me up,
Like the time I was learning to swim and never did,
Clutched you on the first day of kindergarten
Afraid to let go of you.
Now I've let you go
Like you let me go.

When I left you for the last time,
On the airplane home,
I felt two taps on the shoulder,
Thought it was probably some obnoxious kid,
The kind who likes to kick seats.
I turned around
No one was there.
What were you trying to tell me?

My first panic attack
In the connecting airport
I was told my baggage had been sent to a city
Across the country
I thought your things would be lost to me
Never to be reclaimed.
Stood in line waiting for someone to help me
Only to be told there was nothing she could do
She saw me falling
Then took me in a wheelchair to the front of the line
I was told that it had been a mistake.

I even let a man into my body
Because I thought you had sent him to me
To fill the space that you left when you went
I made him into what I wanted him to be.
He took what he wanted, then disappeared
You always said men were only good for one thing
Was this your way of proving it to me?

You kept me tethered to the earth
Made me believe that you would never go
But the one who made me live and lived for me is gone
You gave me the gift of life
I gave you the gift of death
Now I drift unmoored, bereft
Wondering what other ways you will let me know
            that you're not gone—yet.

Pursuit

I went to the woods to find a place for my grief,
Thought I could bury it or leave it behind
for some wild animal to eat.
Instead it ran after me.

I heard the pad of its feet in the leaves,
Felt its fur and flesh when it caught me,
pounced, held me in its teeth
shook me 'til mine rattled
spat me out, threw me on the ground

I lay there, dazed, wondering
what blood it thought it could get out of me.

The Opening

You said to me, *You're so closed up.*
At first, I thought of an abandoned store
A sign on the door denying admittance
The interior dark and dusty with disuse
Any signs of life hidden
From anyone who dared to peer in
A combination of neglect and disinterest.

Then I thought of a peony,
A perfect sphere, its petals overlapping
Like arms folded, held tightly to the chest
Protecting the heart like a bulletproof vest
Then the bursting that no one sees
But seems to happen magically
When the packed bud unfolds,
Spreads its petals to open itself
To whatever may sip from its nectar.

Confidence Man

You came in your wagon
Stood on my doorstep
Surveyed the devastation
Opened your bag
Showed me rocks you'd dug up
Read me poems you'd written
Sea glass you found on a beach
I thought you'd been sent
by the mother who had left me.

You opened your bottle
Told me you had a remedy
To heal me
Put your fingers
On and in my body
As if you could draw out the demons
Lured me in with your slippery words,
Your slithery tongue.

You opened your hand
Flim flam man
Showed me fool's gold
Counterfeit money
Made me buy into your scam
A fake, a phony
You put the make on me.
You stood outside the carnival tent
Told me of the wonders within
Sights I'd never seen or would see again
Waved your hand
Said step right up
Beckoned me to go in.

All I found was a hall of mirrors
My image reflected
Projected through a lens of grief.
The glass shattered and
 I picked up the shards
Cut myself on the edges of lies
Tried to put them back together
Put the snake back in the bottle
The artifacts back into the carpetbag
And send you back to where you really came from.

The Scent of a Woman

When I told you that I was going on a hike
You said to watch out for deer,
That a woman had been gored by one
Simply because it was attracted to her scent.

I found a single incident of this.
A transgender woman in Glasgow
Punctured in the neck
When a trapped deer ran at her in what was called
A freak accident.

I think of you as that stag
You smelled vulnerability
Ran at me to escape your own body
Silence the voice that said you couldn't be free
Penetrated me to heal yourself
Left me to bandage my own wounds.

Karma

A woman scorned
She keeps score
Makes hash marks and slash marks
Every slight recorded

She keeps a tally
Counts the number
Just when you think you've outrun her
She'll stick out her foot and trip you
Burn bridges behind you
Build bridges before you.

She's the one you done wrong
The one who sings a song
Of revenge
A lament for what might have been.

That time you thought you would have some fun,
Take the trust of someone who needed to believe,
Use it for your own amusement,
Then disappear and laugh from afar?

She knows where you are
Won't rest until you get
what you deserve
Just when you think you're safe.

Distillation

I'm not aging like a fine wine, getting better with age.
I have no floral notes or complex aromas
No fruit forward flavors of peach or mango
No savory flavors of sage or quince
My body profile is not full but flabby,
My finish is not smooth but bitter.
I am more like vinegar or whiskey
Not single malt but sour mash
With spent mash used from an older batch
Yeast and acid bubbling
Water, malt, barley, corn
Corrosive enough to burn the cauldron
Yet hitting the palate with a note of woodsmoke
A hint of leather, and a touch of arsenic.

Into the Woods

Into the woods
        like Little Red Riding Hood
Then into a clearing
        with a choice of two paths
Should I take the path of needles or pins?
The trees part and the path is clear, level
Crickets hop beside me
Butterflies flutter in front of me
The path dips and turns, past the refinery,
        back into the woods, benches placed along the way
I stop to rest, watch cyclists whizz past,
Start walking again, hear the whoosh of bikes behind me.
A boy says, "What are you doing here? Just walking?"
I ignore him and walk on.
A man with his dog tells me some boys are further down the path and
        I might want to watch them.
The path dips again, and I see four of them
        forming a barrier with their bikes, daring me to pass
I try to burst them into flames with my eyes.
The bikes part, and we go our separate ways.

Midlife Crisis

Cresting the hill of 50 years old,
I wish I were there already
Half a century behind me and another ahead of me
I peer into the mirror
Pluck stray hairs
Look for gray hairs
Leave them in
My hair is getting thin
Receding from my forehead
Where acne still lingers
I miss the Tamoxifen
Power surges
Periods that were
More like commas
Now it's back to the cramping and bloating
Desperation for chocolate at three in the morning
I want more lines on my face
Grooves in the road to show where I've been
Pockmarks like potholes
I don't want a sports car but a Sherman tank
Not a boy toy, but a joy toy,
One that swivels, lights up, plays "The Stars and Stripes Forever"
I want to be left alone to grow old.

My Earlier Self

I like to think I'm hip and with it,
Radical even,
A live-and-let-live kind of gal.
Same-sex marriage? No problem.
Late-term abortion? Nobody's business.
But the smallest thing will set me off,
A "No problem" instead of a "You're welcome,"
Children walking across my lawn,
Someone standing in the middle of the aisle,
         trying to decide which ketchup to buy.

I wonder if I was brought back from another time,
My earlier self the kind of woman who never smiled
         for photographs
Or laughed when someone told a bawdy joke,
Her corset laced a little too tight and a horsehair bustle
         that made her itch.

Ceremony

The lamps have been lit.
She sets out her instruments.
This is the one that will make the cut quick.
This is the one that will suture it.
These are the pincers to pull the skin.
This is the pan to put it in
       once it is released from its home.
This woman operates alone,
       removes pieces of herself to feel whole.

Holly Norton spent her formative years in Iowa and has degrees from Luther College, Iowa State University, and Bowling Green State University. She is a professor at the University of Northwestern Ohio and teaches composition, communication, and other courses that she has developed, such as Myth and Fairy Tales, Gothic Literature, and Women Who Rock. She is a member of the American Association of University Women, the Emily Dickinson International Society, and the Academy of American Poets. Norton is president of the Northwest Ohio Literacy Council Board of Trustees; a volunteer for Family Promise, an organization dedicated to helping homeless families find housing; and Churches United Pantry, an organization dedicated to maintaining a food pantry for those in need. Reading and traveling are her passions. She has been to 21 countries and plans to visit more.